THE
COLOUR
OF
CANADA

THE
COLOUR
OF
CANADA

text by

HUGH MACLENNAN

The Canadian Illustrated Library

Contents

The Canadian Illustrated Library

McClelland and Stewart Limited,

ILLUSTRATED BOOKS DIVISION.
150 Simcoe Street, Toronto 1, Ont., Canada.

PUBLISHER: Jack McClelland
EDITORIAL DIRECTOR: Pierre Berton
CREATIVE DIRECTOR: Frank Newfeld
EDITOR: Leslie F. Hannon
ART DIRECTOR: Keith Scott
PICTURE EDITOR: Prudence Hemelrijk
EXECUTIVE ASSISTANT: Ennis Halliday

Hugh MacLennan

The author of this book is, at 60, Canada's most-distinguished novelist.
Born in the Maritimes, he won a Rhodes scholarship and studied at Oxford
and, later, at Princeton. He is now Associate Professor of English at McGill
University. His great contribution to Canadian literature has been recognized
by the conferment of honorary degrees, and, in 1953, he was elected a
Fellow of the Royal Society. He has been given Governor-General's Awards
for his novels, Two Solitudes and The Precipice and for a collection of
his essays. He will publish his sixth novel, Return of the Sphinx in 1967.

..."This land
is far more important
than we are.
To know it
is to be young
and ancient
all at once."

M OST of the pictures in this book are of
the Canadian land, a land larger than
any one person can hope to comprehend, but con-
taining what is still a very small nation. The land,
of course, will last as long as the world does, but
the nation is only a tenant on it.

How long the present tenant's lease will run
depends upon more than the nation's people. The
land is rich and magnificent; since the climate has
grown warmer, it is much more attractive than it
used to be. Everyone knows how overcrowded the
world is getting and that the so-called rights of
nations weigh little against hunger, greed, power
and the need for living space. But at the moment
the land is still presumed to belong to the people
who live on it.

In 1967 I can write of Canada, the nation, only
if I write personally. I can't give myself the illusion
of being sure of many things anymore. Certain facts,
knowledges, observations, intuitions – armed and
often confused by these, one lives in a world that is
almost but not quite out of human control, its ac-
cumulated information so vast that everyone knows

he is ignorant, its technical communications so efficient that it has been called an electronic village, the new phrase for a technologically created Babel. We try to come to terms with material power such as there never was matched by an individual certainty of soul unparalleled on such a scale since the Black Death. A new age is a-borning; it is probably here. But nobody I have met or read understands it, and not many even pretend to.

If anyone disagrees with this picture of human society in 1967, I can only hope that he is right and that I am wrong. At the moment this is my view of it and the view with which I am writing. Canada is now celebrating the hundredth anniversary of her existence as a so-called independent nation, and nothing has been more typical of her than the way she contrives to exist despite determined efforts on the part of pundits to prove that she has no right to, that she makes no sense economically, politically or scientifically. Neither does a giraffe – a thought I find comforting. Canada is not a logical construction. She never was, and I have the idea that if she ever tries to be logical about herself she will rationalize away her existence. Some of her citizens are trying to do so now. But for the time being, she still seems to prefer the inconsistencies of life to the precisions of logic and proved it with unusual clarity as she neared her hundredth birthday.

A few years ago the young men of the Quebec separatist movement were looking forward to 1967 not as the anniversary year of the nation's birth but as the nation's funeral. Mysteriously, on the eve of the Centennial, the movement died down to a few scattered whimpers. Then some strong-jawed men west of the Laurentian Shield began to mutter (though less publicly) that two could play at the separatist game. They had the oil – or did Americans have it? They had the water and potash – or did Americans want it? They had a great Pacific port – so why not go it alone? But the West also

prepared for the Centennial. And in Quebec, at the height of the separatist activities, Mayor Jean Drapeau bid for and obtained the International Exhibition of 1967 and the theme of it ("*Terre des Hommes* – Man and His World") seems more pertinent to the times than the "Century Of Progress Exhibition" which opened in New York in 1939, when the progress it celebrated reached another of its many climaxes with the outbreak of the Second World War.

"Political unity seems the last thing the Canadian people want now . . ."

Politically, Canada prepared for her Centennial by holding a series of indecisive elections which left the central government, the very seat of Confederation, almost weaker than the strongest provinces. Political unity as it is understood elsewhere seems the last thing the Canadian people want now, though they always assert that it is their greatest need. Is this intelligent? Obviously not, but it occurs to me that it may be something better.

"*Il est bon,*" wrote a French philosopher, "*et plus souvent qu'on ne le pense, de savoir de n'avoir pas de l'esprit.*" A good thing not to be intelligent? The spirit of the whole century laughs at such an idea. Yet it is a fact that many a plain man has been asking just what good the super-brains of our epoch have been doing for humanity lately. Hot wars and cold wars, H-bombs and the vehicles to deliver them, from one continent to another, revolutions and counter-revolutions, propaganda and Madison Avenue, a super-colossal technology harnessed to produce the one condition of life which man has always found intolerable – leisure. The most brilliantly intelligent minds of the age have occupied themselves with these activities to the virtual exclusion of everything else.

But Canada is not a brilliant nation and one of the few things that seem reasonably clear to me, if to nobody else, is that by pure instinct (there can be no other explanation) we are once more reasserting the historic decision of the nation's founders to stand as aloof as we can afford to from the present obsessions and drives of our mighty and friendly neighbour, though of course we never say this publicly. Just how aloof that can be is one of those nice calculations dear to the Canadian soul: all the American investment we can get, but not too much American investment; economic union with the States but not necessarily economic union; recognition of Red China but not necessarily recognition. O Canada, with such subtleties as these we stand on guard for thee!

> "The United States
> is quite
> the most marvellous
> country
> in the world."

We all know that the Canadian nation – informal questionnaires put by myself to McGill undergraduates satisfy me that at least 9% of us know it – came into being because our ancestors repudiated the most important single event in the history of the western hemisphere, the American Revolution. Canada exists today because they said no to that. She will cease to exist if she ever says yes to that, unless she does so in the spirit of a girl in the back seat of a taxi with one eye on the meter and the other on the profile of the determined man who took her out that night.

Just the same, that decision of our ancestors has haunted their descendants ever since. The United States is quite the most marvellous country in the world. She became so rich, successful, exciting and proud, and for years her public pleasure in herself was an enchantment. The ideals on which she was founded rang like bugles around the globe. Her techniques were copied everywhere, and in no countries more meticulously than in Canada and the Soviet Union.

No wonder the descendants of the original Loyalists, looking enviously across the border the British had so negligently agreed to accept for them, asked themselves whether their ancestors had not ruined their children's lives by betting them on the wrong horse. Even some French Canadians thought the same. Calixa Lavalée, the author of our national anthem, was one of them. He left Canada, became an American citizen and from New York sent pamphlets home urging his former country men to follow his example. Nor was there ever a lack of those who did. Successive generations were depleted by hundreds of thousands – millions would be no exaggeration – of energetic and able men and women who gravitated like iron filings to the magnet and were lost to Canada.

Nearly everyone called Canada negative in her growing years, and so she was. The only way it seemed possible for French Canada to survive was to make Quebec a virtual reservation, repudiating the value of nearly everything that had happened since 1763. English Canada clung with pathetic loyalty to the fading glories of a Britain that had little interest in her except in time of war or a royal visit. Worse was yet to come. In the twentieth century the final death of the British Empire coincided with the swamping of our information-media by those of the United States, and the old frustration of the baffled horse-player changed into a kind of guilt-neurosis, as though by staying Canadians (and therefore not being Americans) we were defying the will of God. For the Americans were serious when they called the United States "God's Own Country. "They still are. "The tremendous prosperity, power and blessing," writes Billy Graham, "which America has enjoyed through the years came because we as a nation honoured God. It is, I believe, a direct fulfilment of the promise, 'Blessed is the nation whose God is the Lord.' "

But with stubborn negation, often against their conscious minds, the majority of us shied away from Manifest Destiny even after we had been trained to judge our worth solely as we saw it reflected in the eyes of our neighbours. This meant that whenever we boasted about anything, we boasted about our real estate, raw materials, wheat, scenery and Mounted Police, these being the only things Canadian that interested our neighbours. Until, perhaps, recently.

Our destiny, so we were told occasionally by our more optimistic politicians, always lay in some distant future and never was defined. Sir Wilfrid Laurier uttered the famous prediction that just as the nineteenth century had belonged to the United States, so would the twentieth belong to Canada. Bold statements of this sort are so rare in Canada that this particular one found its way into most of our school books, though anyone who took a good look at it must have known how absurd it was. The nineteenth century never "belonged" to the United States; if it belonged to anyone it belonged to Britain, which cashed in during those years on her victory over France and her headstart in the Industrial Revolution. As for the twentieth century, from 1914 until the first Russian sputnik it clearly "belonged" to the United States, which cashed in on the decline of Europe and her own brilliance in business and technology. But the twentieth century is not over yet. Possibly, though in a sense very different from the one intended by Laurier, at least some of it may be shared by Canada if we have the nerve to follow the instinct of the nation's founders and translate it into a rational purpose.

"We will have set an example to other peoples . . ."

A nation can become valuable to mankind only if it succeeds in co-operating with what might be called an historical need. For the first time Canada may have a chance of doing that. If we can resolve our own confusions here at home, we will have done more than make Canada a happier and more fruitful country than she is now. We will have set an example to other peoples confused and battered, pulled hither and thither by the struggle and obsessions of the two super-powers.

Let's look backward and ask ourselves frankly what actually were the reasons why the original Canadians repudiated the American Revolution. To understand them might help us to make up our minds today. The usual explanations are that the Loyalists were Tories hostile to liberty and progress, while the French Canadian Church abominated democracy worse than the Vatican used to abominate Communism. But surely these explanations are superficial. Why should a French Canada abandoned by such a miserable practicing Catholic as Louis xv, owing neither him nor France an adulterated *sou*, the Union Jack of their conquerors flying over British garrisons in their own cities, have said no to the Americans when they revolted against Britain? The reason was basic; it was not intelligent but visceral. They wanted to survive *as a people*, and it was as simple as that. If they said yes to the Revolution, they would prosper more as individuals in their material lives, but as a people they would disappear and lose all sense of themselves as such.

Why did the Loyalists, most of whom deplored the stupidity and corruption of Lord North's government, refuse to join the Revolution? Certainly not because they were anti-democratic or afraid of losing their privileges. Very few of them were rich and privileged, and if they had been hostile to democracy they never would have introduced the town meeting into Ontario and the Maritime Provinces, nor would their sons have struggled for responsible government in British North America until, without a revolution or severing their ties with the motherland, they won it.

What does all this mean unless it means that what the French Canadians and the Loyalists were rejecting was something deeper than was visible on the surface? Letters and statements made by Loyalists suggest that they knew very well what it was. It was not the ideals of the Revolution, but the hidden passions which those ideals masked.

In a famous book written in 1923 (*Studies In Classic American Literature*) D. H. Lawrence writes with a wild and fascinated eloquence about those drives which lay hidden underneath the idealism of the American Revolution, and few learned Americans have denied that he was basically right, especially in recent years when they have to live with the results of them.

Lawrence sought to explain the startling contradiction between the pride and confidence taken by Americans in their wonderful, rationally created nation and the violence, irrationality and unhappiness that have pervaded most of the best American literature from Melville and Hawthorne until the present day. The typical American hero of the deepest American literature is nearly always a defeated *individual*, a desperate man alienated from the triumphant crowd: Captain Ahab striking his harpoons into the whale that symbolized the super-ego of American puritanism and the *Pequod* going down with flag flying, sunk by that same whale which here symbolizes the natural world which the conscious ego had tried to master; the lone American caught by the sheriff's posse and growling, "My name is Sam Hall and I hate you one and all — God damn your eyes!" and now, in most post-war literature, the defiant American hero has merged into the passive anti-hero who can imagine no other role than civil disobedience. Why all this?

Lawrence finds his explanation in the hidden compulsions of many early New Englanders; had he been more familiar with literature south of the Mason and Dixon Line he would have found examples even more striking. Most of the revolutionary Americans, so Lawrence thought, were seeking to escape, to get away. But from what? The ineffectual authority of an ineffectual king who lived in London? And if there was a determination to create a state where all men would enjoy life, liberty and the pursuit of happiness, why did the revolutionaries retain the institution of slavery? Underneath the perfect rationality of the most perfect constitution lurked something hidden, and it was this that the Loyalists rejected.

"But nobody can escape from his past . . ."

Lawrence is right, surely, when he says that what America really sought to escape was nothing less than the human past of Europe — history itself and the long and exhausting burden of it. Under God

"The vastness is deceptive...only 7% could ever be cultivated"

Attungala, a Canadian citizen, strides through the
normal winter ground drift in the arctic highlands.

"More fresh air and water than in any other part of the earth"

The Old Crow country, north-east Yukon Territory.

a new continent, they aspired to create a new and purer nation, uncontaminated by the evil past, free forever from the repetitive patterns of history and injustice. "No foreign entanglements" was echoed a quarter of a century later by Henry Ford's "History is the bunk."

But nobody can escape from his past, neither can any nation live alone and escape from history, as successive American presidents have discovered. The effort to be superior to the past, superior to human nature, is more than human nature can bear, no matter how nobly people try to bear it. As Lawrence saw it, such an effort was bound to alienate the individual, the blood-and-flesh woman and man, and at the same time exalt and magnify the state which, as its power grew, imperceptibly was given the kind of worship and obedience usually offered to God. "Hear ye, O America, our nation is one nation" — and in order to preserve the mystique of its unity, the most humble and merciful of presidents waged the most terrible civil war in history. Now challenged by a newer messianic ideology, the power and concentration of the state has become . . . but these are deep waters, and we have no fishing rights in them.

But we still do have our huge country and our little nation. Nor is it anti-American to emphasize that it was because Canadians had no wish to alienate themselves from the past and from their European source that the Canadian nation came into being.

Earlier I said that this peculiar nation of ours, in most things important, acts from instinct and sentiment. She has always tried to guard her continuities. If to do so is unfashionable, her leaders pay unfailing lip-service to the pressures of the moment, but in practice they seek to guard the continuities. Why else was there such a soul-searching over the ditching of the Red Ensign in favour of a distinctive national flag? Why else does Quebec insist upon the maintenance of her French culture? Our instinct — perhaps in the insanity of the cold war our reason goes along with it — tells us now that the only "unity" worth having is one which will permit the greatest possible variety of individual and collective differences, that the individual will have a chance only if he is given priority over the vast, impersonal state. The world today is on a psychic hinge, and the young generation, confused though it is, everywhere recognizes that the challenge it faces in the Age of Affluence is not a material but a spiritual one. Flesh and blood against the abstraction; genuine human needs against the needs of the power-producing super-organization.

"Our two solitudes may still be solitary, but they have begun to talk with one another."

Therefore I believe that the perennial Canadian "racial" problem is our greatest single asset. Again and again it has prevented us from opting for the kind of unity which turns a government into a huge abstraction. In our own muddled way in this Centennial year — and far beyond it — we are at least trying to provide in Canada a political home for diversity. Our two solitudes may still be solitary, but they have begun to talk with one another. Is it more than wishful-thinking to believe that if Canada succeeds, she will be a pilot-plant for a broader human liberty in this frightened world? Could anything be worse for the over-burdened United States than to have us inflict our problems upon it?

"A land larger than any one person can hope to comprehend"

The Oblate church at Thom Bay, Northwest Territories.

We still have the land; we are still its tenants. The land is our overwhelming common denominator. A land of dramatic contrasts with an undeveloped frontier – much of it probably undevelopable – almost as large as Europe: Great rivers, only a few of them polluted so far; thousands of lakes and three oceans flanking the whole. Stupidly, we overcrowd three urban areas, a buck being still sacred with us. But the plane which leaves Vancouver air terminal flies over virgin mountains within ten or fifteen minutes. The cars streaming out of Montreal and Toronto can usually reach the wilderness in less than two hours. Twenty-five minutes of easy driving can take a Haligonian to an empty shore on a Sunday afternoon. When you stand on a high point in Quebec City you can see, only a few miles away, the ramparts of the Laurentian Shield.

This land is far more important than we are. To know it is to be young and ancient all at once. Its virginity is our visible link with the beginnings of the race and the millions of New Canadians who have come here have found constant reminders of their homes in older countries.

In 1937 when I went through Scandinavia to Russia, I said in Denmark, "But this is like Prince Edward Island"; in Sweden, "How like New Brunswick this is!" In Finland, "Just like Quebec fifteen miles north of the river, or Ontario above Simcoe." In Russia and Poland I thought inevitably of the prairie provinces. A few years ago, sailing from Athens along the coast of Argolis, had I not known I was in the Aegean I could easily have mistaken that rocky shore for the coasts of Cape Breton or Newfoundland. British Columbia is our Norway. And one dawn on the Mackenzie, waking in the wheelhouse of a dredge moored at Wrigley Harbour, the sun striking like a searchlight across the river under a mass of clouds, wild ducks and geese arrowing off the water – this was North America when the first white men saw it!

IN this book we discover Canada somewhat as the explorers, settlers and *voyageurs* discovered it. We begin at the rocky harbours of Newfoundland and Nova Scotia, glance at the gentle farmland of Prince Edward Island in summer and winter, at the old Loyalist city of Saint John and some of the lovely rivers of New Brunswick. We come to Gaspé, go up the St. Lawrence past modern Quebec and Montreal, enter briefly the Eastern Townships, then pass through the water gap leading to the Great Lakes and Ontario. We look at the new Toronto and a variety of scenes in Ontario before leaping across the Shield to the Prairies – space apparently limitless under shifting skies all the way to the Rocky Mountains. We go through the mountains to the coast where a sea bird flies out from the land over the Pacific. The North is still a separate region so far as communications and the life of the people are concerned, and we treat it separately in the pictures in this book.

" . . . the Prairies – a sea of land."

Geographically, Canada consists of five very different regions: first, the Atlantic provinces, glacier-scraped, settled for the most part along the coasts (and in New Brunswick along the rivers), apparently small yet so indented that the coastline of "little" Nova Scotia is some 5,000 miles long – a distance much greater than an air line from Halifax to Victoria; then the nation's core, Quebec-Ontario, bound together despite linguistic differences by the St. Lawrence and Ottawa river systems and the Laurentian Shield; then the Prairies, a sea of land lying between the American border and the arbitrary line of the Northwest Territories; then the Cordilleran West; finally the North. This latter region consists really of more than the Yukon, the

Abandoned at Lake Bennett, an old wooden church
recalls the stampeders who roared by
on their way to Dawson City and the Klondike.

Northwest Territories and the islands of the Arctic Ocean; along Hudson Strait, Ungava Bay and northern Labrador it overlaps Quebec.

" . . . a culture of cities
like a
colossal ancient
Greece."

Canada's geographical vastness is deceptive. At the moment little more than 4% of the whole country is under cultivation; it has been estimated that only 7% ever can be. All indications point to a country where, apart from the Prairies, the population will be congregated in a number of densely populated areas suitable for trade and industry: in short, a culture of cities like a colossal ancient Greece, with nature picturesque and largely unspoiled just outside them, a country as different as could be imagined from the United States with its rich parklands and thousands of small market towns.

The contrast between the geographical and human maps of Canada is startling, as can be seen if we compare her to Great Britain.

The land area of the main British island is some 5,000 square miles smaller than that of the combined Atlantic provinces; the British population is 30 times greater. Quebec-Ontario is eleven times larger than Britain; the population is only a quarter as large. The Prairies exceed Britain in area by a ratio of 6.5; Britain's population exceeds theirs by 20-1. The corresponding ratios of land and population in British Columbia and the North are, respectively, 4-1 and 1-45; 16.5 to 1 and 1-250!

It has often been estimated that by the year 2,000 A.D. the total Canadian population will touch 40 millions, but we make no predictions about that here, remembering that in 1930 the experts predicted that by 1960 the population of the United States would level off at 145 millions. The present population explosion can easily be arrested in the Western nations and already there are indications that a falling-off has commenced. The only prediction we do make here is that the central Mackenzie Basin will be more heavily populated than it is now: the country is beautiful and the mean temperatures in the region of Fort Simpson are higher than they were at Quebec City a century ago. If mosquitos and blackflies can be controlled, this would be one of the finest lands anyone could wish to inhabit.

"Can we not
at last say
yes
to this land?"

A culture of cities with unspoiled nature in abundance, more fresh air and water than in any other part of the earth – if only our imaginations could look both back and forward, back to the loveliness of the cities of ancient Greece and forward to what such a combination of urbanity and the wilderness promises us!

Can we not at last say yes to this land the ancient navigators discovered for us and the *voyageurs* opened up for us? Changes in the climate have made it easier for us than for the pioneers, but it still is a dramatic climate. If it becomes soft and tropical it is never for long. A storm breaks and astringent air pours in from the north to blow away the smog we still believe is allowable because there is temporary profit in it for those who make it. The sky is electric blue and old men remember their youth. This land is too precious to be put at auction.

Midnight in May near the Arctic Circle.

The journey begins:

The Maritimes

Look at the art of the sea, how it shapes and
polishes granite. Feel its cold cleanness; its power
when it thunders against the land in a whole
gale. If you stood on the rocks of Peggy's Cove on
a day like this you would be in danger. If the
camera had been turned inland you would see spume
like thin snow rushing across a rising moor
of stunted trees with granite tors standing like
prehistoric monsters. Just behind this rock lies
the famous cove with little fishing boats,
jetties piled with lobster pots, white cottages and
a church. On fine days you can sit here in the
sun with your back propped against North America
and your eyes ranging over a sea that extends
uninterrupted to old Guyenne and Gascony.

OPPOSITE: PEGGY'S COVE, NOVA SCOTIA

A tiny outport in Newfoundland where
men of the Caucasian race have
lived in the New World longer than
anywhere above the Rio Grande
or below the Spanish Main. Poetic
names, haunting or majestic,
redolent of history: Heart's Content,
Seldom-Come-By, Blow-Me-Down
(a corruption of Blomidon, the old
navigator), Port Aux Basques
(here Basque fishermen dried their
catches before taking them home);
Bonavista Bay, Conception Bay,
Placentia Bay, Avalon. Only a few years
ago in these regions people spoke
in the accents of Shakespeare's England.

Newfoundland has been always a
stepping stone between the
hemispheres. Vikings were here before
Cabot; Englishmen, Frenchmen,
Spaniards, Portuguese shared the
fishing rights before the
Pilgrims landed in Massachusetts.
The Labrador Current washes
the island, makes it chilly and foggy;
the storms are terrifying.
Steamers following the Great Circle
from New York to Europe pass
in sight of Cape Race, and the Titanic
was only the most famous of
the ones that failed to finish the voyage.
In little boats like these
the fishermen of Newfoundland put out
to the rescue in North Atlantic
winter gales. Alcock and Brown left
Newfoundland in 1919 on the
first non-stop trans-Atlantic flight.
In the Hitler War, Gander
was the last airport of Ferry Command.
Now, after centuries of heroic
isolation, Newfoundland is part of
Canada, and the continent,
the oldest and newest province.

HIBBS' HOLE, NEWFOUNDLAND

St. John's wind-swept, rain-washed houses — warm and comfortable, wonderful houses to grow up in like those of Saint John, N.B., today and of Halifax before Halifax lifted its face after the Hitler War. The finest wines drunk in North America are drunk in St. John's. Here, too, is played some of North America's shrewdest politics — politics can only be real where people know each other in the bones and the blood corpuscles, otherwise they are illusions called "images." A city that a while ago was almost a city-state. It was from Signal Hill in St. John's that Marconi sent his first trans-Atlantic wireless message. It was here, too, that Premier Joey Smallwood broke the last Family Compact in North America.

TERRA NOVA NATIONAL PARK, NEWFOUNDLAND

LEFT: ST. JOHN'S, NEWFOUNDLAND

If the population explosion continues, people will be eating seaweed like this—or food products manufactured from it. Now the weed nourishes mussels, periwinkles and spiny sea-urchins. A little way inland the rocks are stained here and there with violet daubs made by urchins caught by gulls and dropped to break their shells.

MAHONE BAY, NOVA SCOTIA

A mid-Victorian office building molders in downtown Halifax a few steps away from the classically beautiful Province Building where Joseph Howe presided over the first responsible government in British North America, and two minutes from the docks of the inner harbour.

ON GRANVILLE STREET, HALIFAX, NOVA SCOTIA

Halifax, founded by Cornwallis in 1749 as a naval
and military base against Louisbourg, is one
of the three finest natural harbours in the world.
It was the greatest convoy base in the two
World Wars of our century and before that, as a
base of the Royal Navy, it knew the
admirals from Boscawen through Nelson to Fisher.
The famous Citadel is now a museum.

Lunenburg County was settled by Protestant
Germans immediately after the founding
of Halifax. They are the oldest Canadians after
the French, but the German language
has disappeared. Old German names like Weinacht
are now spelled Whynot; Eisenhauer has
become Isnor and, by a wonderful transformation,
Bübickhöfer is now Publicover. The
Lunenburgers were the last professional seamen
under sail; Bluenose, their most famous
ship, is remembered on the Canadian ten cent piece.

RIGHT: BLUE ROCK, NEAR LUNENBURG,
       NOVA SCOTIA

BELOW: HALIFAX, AS SEEN FROM DARTMOUTH,
       NOVA SCOTIA

Louisbourg in Cape Breton
Island — once the loneliest,
foggiest, most expensively
fortified outpost of any
European power in North
America. Garrisoned by
French troops, ill-defended
by the French Navy,
unsupported by such habitant
colonists as made the defence
of Quebec an epic, Louisbourg
fell to Britain and the
New Englanders in the War
of the Austrian Succession,
was restored to France
when the war ended and was
re-fortified at such cost
that Louis XV complained
that he would soon see
the bastions of Louisbourg
rising over the horizon.
The city fell for the second
and last time in the Seven
Years' War and this opened
Wolfe's way to Quebec.
The British razed city and
fortifications to the
ground and left the site to
the fogs and seagulls.
Now the Canadian government
is rebuilding its most
impressive structures as a
national monument. These
anchors, once belonging to
eighteenth century ships
of the line, were dredged from
the bottom of Louisbourg
Harbour by the Dominion
Coal Company.

LOUISBOURG, NOVA SCOTIA

A few hundred yards from where this bridge stands occurred the Halifax Explosion, December 6, 1917.

THE DARTMOUTH-HALIFAX BRIDGE, NOVA SCOTIA

The Cabot Trail. — No scenic highway in North America compresses into such a short length (188 miles) such an astonishing variety: cliffs, ocean vistas, highland glens, river meadows and a short stretch of the Bras d'Or Lakes. Frigid seas and grayish-pink granite on the Atlantic shore; along the Gulf of St. Lawrence, Sienna-red cliffs and warm water in summer, Mediterranean light on fine days and, from Cap Rouge, a view like the one from Taormina on the eastern coast of Sicily. The people are mostly of Highland Scottish or French ancestry and even now some Gaelic and French lingers.

BESIDE THE CABOT TRAIL, CAPE BRETON ISLAND, NOVA SCOTIA

Not all the Maritimes are stern and rocky; Prince Edward Island is almost a garden, famous for its potatoes, dairy products, the straightforward honesty of its people, its bathing beaches, its superb Malpeque oysters and Anne of Green Gables.

HUNTER RIVER VALLEY, PRINCE EDWARD ISLAND

The gentle island lies in the path of nor'easters from Labrador bringing blizzards in winter and drift ice in the spring which chokes the harbours. They talk hopefully of a causeway across Northumberland Strait. Will all Cape Breton Island hold enough rock for it?

SUMMERFIELD, PRINCE EDWARD ISLAND

Saint John, N.B. was settled by Loyalists who arrived in
convoys in 1783; some of them were buried in this
graveyard in the city's heart. A fine harbour with a great
sea-faring tradition — here the White Star Line was
born. The Reversing Falls of the St. John River (caused
by the huge Fundy tide) divide the city from the
suburb of Lancaster. Saint John has been called the most
conservative city in Canada. It probably is.

CHURCHYARD, SAINT JOHN, NEW BRUNSWICK

A Victorian hotel of the kind that has disappeared
almost everywhere except in New Brunswick. Most
of old Loyalist Saint John perished in the fire of
1877 which gutted the city's heart. This was
the worst architectural loss in Canada's history,
for rebuilding was done in a hurry, much of
it in the red brick style of the late Victorian era.

ROYAL HOTEL, SAINT JOHN, NEW BRUNSWICK

New Brunswick is a land of rivers,
all of them beautiful and
none gigantic. Rich farms and quiet
market towns grew slowly
along the banks of the St. John,
Kennebecasis and Peticodiac and
some of the old houses are
jewels. Fredericton is surely one of
the most dignified little cities
in North America, with an
exquisite cathedral and our oldest
university. Until recently,
the St. John was the best salmon
river on the eastern side of
the continent. The dam at Beechwood,
soon to be followed by still
another dam, has reduced the salmon
somewhat, and changed the pattern
of life on the river. But great
rafts of lumber still come down from
northern New Brunswick
and northern Maine and form masses
of bobbing logs several miles
square at Maugerville. This was the
country where Sir Charles
G. D. Roberts wrote his nature
stories. In the northeast of the province
the Miramichi and the Restigouche
are famous salmon streams still.

A RIVERSIDE HAMLET,
NEW BRUNSWICK

The waterscapes of Nova Scotia

Bridgewater, Nova Scotia

Neil's Harbour, Nova Scotia

Pembroke, Nova Scotia

Blue Rock, Nova Scotia

Port Williams, Nova Scotia

Into Quebec

When national and provincial borders were established in North America at the end of the Eighteenth Century, the decisive factor was often the movement of flowing water. Madawaska County in northern New Brunswick has a panhandle jutting into Maine because the St. John River flows into the Atlantic. The height of land between New Brunswick and Quebec is shared on the principle that such parts as drain into the Atlantic belong to New Brunswick, while those that drain into the St. Lawrence are in Quebec.

Human flows obey no such geographic laws. Northern New Brunswick is mostly French-speaking today because thousands of French Canadians seeped over the height of land to work in the forests and lumber plants of New Brunswick, or to fish the waters along the shore of the St. Lawrence Gulf. St. Leonard and Edmundston are now as "French" as La Tuque. But along the Gulf Shore, many of the French-speaking New Brunswickers are of the Acadian stock which has been there for centuries.

North-eastern New Brunswick is forest land
threaded by famous rivers: the Miramichi, the
Restigouche and the Matapedia which abound in
salmon and feed millions of logs down to the
sawmills and pulp companies at the estuaries. The
Trans-Canada Highway, leaving Edmundston, mounts
slowly up past Lake Temiscouta and descends the
height of land to reach the St. Lawrence at Rivière du
Loup, which looks across to the mountains stretching
north-east from Murray Bay. The other road,
paralleled by the tracks of the C.N.R., skirts
Bay Chaleur with a magnificent view of the Gaspé
mountains, then winds through a hundred miles of the
Matapedia Valley and reaches the St. Lawrence just
below Father Point, where the out-going vessels ship
their pilots. Here the St. Lawrence is only nominally a
river; it is really a firth of the sea—salt water deep
enough to enable German submarines to operate in it
during 1942, cold winds from the icebergs trapped
in Belle Isle, and sometimes schools of white porpoises
playing about the cutwaters of hurrying ships.

Into Quebec

Opposite this rock Jacques Cartier is said to have landed
for the first time on what now is Canadian soil and to have
celebrated Mass on the beach. Percé village (behind the
camera) faces it and a few miles seaward is the bird
sanctuary of Bonaventure Island — a colony of gulls, gannets
and puffins that dive for fish in the frigid water.

PERCÉ ROCK, QUEBEC

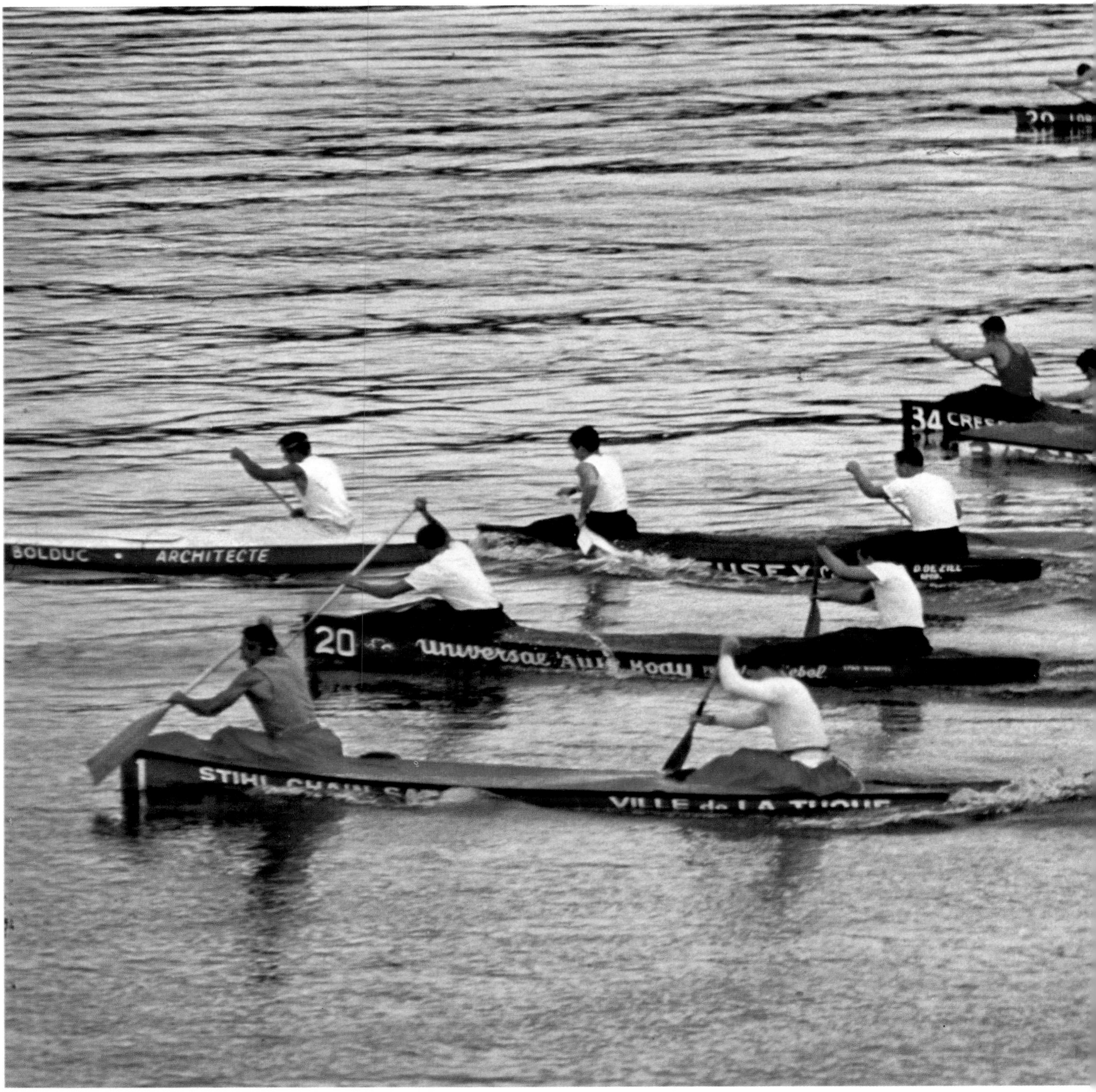
BOLDUC • ARCHITECTE
20
34

The St. Maurice follows a long, rough course through
the timberland to join the St. Lawrence at Trois Rivières,
birthplace of La Vérendrye and Maurice Duplessis.
On this river, Intendant Jean Talon introduced from France
into the New World the practice of driving logs. It is
still one of the most important lumber streams on the continent.

ST. MAURICE RIVER, QUEBEC

The cradle of Canada: Quebec City. Older than Boston by
some twenty-two years, Quebec has always been close to
history's heart. Champlain founded it, New France was
governed from it, epochal events have centred on men
who were associated with it: Frontenac, Laval, Montcalm,
Wolfe, Dorchester, Benedict Arnold, Nelson.
Here in 1943 Winston Churchill and Franklin Roosevelt
with their generals, admirals and airmen made the
final plans for the Normandy Invasion of June 6, 1944.

ABOVE: THE CITADEL, QUEBEC CITY;
RIGHT: LOWER TOWN, QUEBEC CITY

QUEBEC CITY, QUEBEC

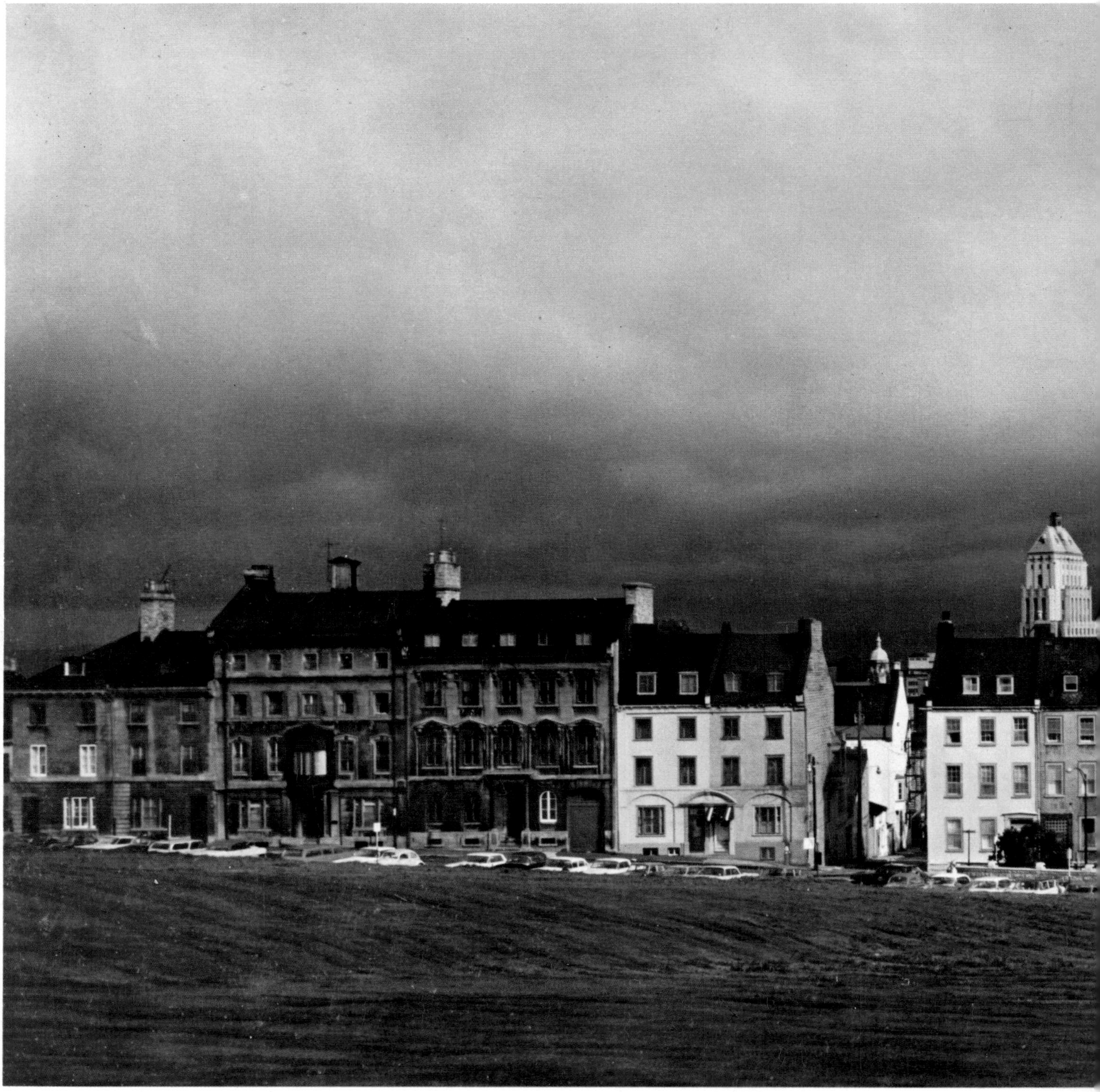

These eighteenth century French provincial houses are near the field where was fought a battle which had the most ironic results in the history of the world. It was won by the British in order to gain for their American colonists the water-entrance to the Ohio Valley. Soon afterwards, the colonists, freed at last from fear of invasion from the north, revolted against their motherland and formed the United States. The defenders of Quebec's Citadel repulsed the American invaders, and in 1783, when the Treaty of Versailles acknowledged the United States as an independent nation, the Union Jack flew over the Citadel the British had taken in order to incorporate the whole of North America into the British Empire. A lesson for us today, perhaps: nothing important has ever happened in Canada the way the planners and experts expected.

The "new" Montreal, French
au fond but in spirit the most
international city in North America,
New York not forgotten.
An empire city (though without an
empire) because of its
location at one of the strategic
points of commerce and
the movements of people. Violently
dramatic in climate,
Montreal can be hotter than
Singapore and as cold
as the Arctic, as smoggy as
London used to be and
electrically vibrant with
glittering skies when
the northern fronts reassert
themselves. Almost as
criminal as Chicago, yet a city
of belfries in which the
angelus rings as in the Middle
Ages. Half a century ago
described as "an English garrison
surrounded by an overgrown
French village", it is now a
metropolis within one
step of becoming a megalopolis,
a seaport with ski-
slopes an hour and a half away
from its skyscrapers.

DORCHESTER BOULEVARD,
MONTREAL, QUEBEC

John de Visser's camera story from the intriguing streets of Montreal

Cities are like water: they seek their own levels. If located on plains, they spread formlessly like water in a marsh. If constrained by nature or walls, they concentrate their forces into a tension at the core. Montreal lies on an island in a river with a mountain in its centre, so her core is concentrated.

Here are the old, the new, the powerful, the helpless, the chic and the chi-chi, reality and illusion for a precarious moment linked in a bizarre harmony, ugliness not yet triumphant, ordinariness threatening everywhere but still held in check.

This column to Horatio Lord Nelson, situated just above Place Jacques Cartier, is older than the one in London's Trafalgar Square.

This confection stands where only a few years ago lived the inheritors of the Victorian upper-middle-class de l'expression Anglaise. Are the original owners apoplectic in their graves?

Classic transition: Upper-middle-class mansion to lower-class rooming house to everyone's-class "maison de rendezvous" – "a boutique".

On winter evenings the cruciform forty-five storey Royal Bank Building shines like a gigantic ice palace. Underneath it are fifty shops, eight restaurants and one of the finest bookshops in the world; about it, the expanse of Place Ville Marie.

Gothic Notre-Dame keeps her stern watch on the Place d'Armes bustle.

Le Sieur de Maisonneuve, the city's founder, still presides defiantly.

It is called le Reine Elizabeth; French is a very subtle language.

The rain reflects the Cathedral of St. Mary Queen of the World, where Dorchester verges on Place Ville Marie. Montreal can still merge into dream; may she always. Quiet amid the new skyscrapers, life-sized images of the Twelve Apostles standing on its pediment, the cathedral rests. At all hours of the day people go quietly in to pray and come quietly out again: sins and remissions of a multitude.

Montrealers thought for years that the
Place des Arts would never be
built, but built it was under the
dynamic leadership of Mayor Jean Drapeau
and it is one of the finest concert
halls in existence; also, a core
of order in a slowly disappearing slum.

PLACE DES ARTS, MONTREAL, QUEBEC

Bonsecours is the most beloved church in
Montreal. Often called the Sailors'
Chapel, it is filled for early morning
Mass by seamen, dockworkers and
the people who have brought their goods
to the nearby market. In its rear,
a statue of St. Ann with outstretched
arms blesses the harbour.

NOTRE-DAME DE BONSECOURS,
MONTREAL, QUEBEC

*It has been said that Quebec's
Eastern Townships remind
everyone of some other place
they know and love. This
region was originally marked out
by Lord Dorchester as land
for Loyalists from New England.
The descendants of the old
settlers still speak in Yankee
twangs, but now the region
is predominately French-speaking
as French Canadians have
moved in from more crowded areas
to farm the land. Hence
some of the place names: Saint-
Adolfe de Dudswell, St. Paul
d'Abbotsford, Stukeley Sud and
Ham Sud. Americans have
called the Townships "a
geographical extension
of New England" — it depends upon
the point of view. There are
splendid lakes like Massawippi,
Memphramagog, Orford.
Hills like the one here, very many
of them, almost but not
quite mountains, loom over the
pasture lands and farms
and in the autumn they blaze or
glow with the scarlet of
maples, the yellow of birches,
the copper of oaks, the
pastel russet-red of butternuts.
The St. Francis is the
principal river and on its banks
is the third largest city
in Quebec. Sherbrooke, once
centred on an English
garrison (when Lord Palmerston
became Colonial Secretary
his first order was to strengthen
it against a possible
American invasion) is now largely
French-speaking.*

HAM SUD,
EASTERN TOWNSHIPS, QUEBEC

The Ottawa River, flowing from one lake into and through another, the only river in Canada whose length it is impossible to determine, the border between Quebec and Ontario, drained the Great Lakes before a geological cataclysm created the Upper St. Lawrence. A century and a half ago, it made possible the timber empire of eastern Canada.

OTTAWA RIVER, THE QUEBEC-ONTARIO BOUNDARY

Up in the Laurentians

The Laurentians are best in winter,
and in Montreal "going north"
means "going ski-ing."
But before the ski-ing, French
Canadians hacked farms
out of the rare patches of arable land
in this Shield country
and built their parishes, with
simple churches like this
one in St. Faustin.

Ontario

There is no dramatic geographic division between Quebec and Ontario because both provinces are dominated by the St. Lawrence River System and the Laurentian Shield. Along and above the shores of Lakes Ontario and Erie, in the Niagara Peninsula and in the larger peninsula terminating at the Detroit and St. Clair Rivers, the Ontario land is much richer than the land in Quebec and more extensively farmed: hence the greater number of small towns and cities. But farther north the Shield country is much the same in both provinces.

The real division is ethnic and historical, Quebec having been settled by French-speaking Roman

Catholics, Ontario by Protestant Loyalists later reinforced by Protestant Scots and Irish, with the consequence that for a long time Europe's old religious rivalries continued in Canada. This particular outlet for human stupidity is now far less important than it was. "French" and "English" may still be two solitudes, but at least they are now learning to respect one another. Their joint ownership of the land makes this necessary, just as, a century ago, it made it necessary for them to form a political union. They knew that if they could not hang together, they would hang separately.

Ontario

Ottawa was the most unlikely spot
anyone could imagine for a
national capital. A century ago it
was an over-grown lumber village
noted for its drunken brawls
and cholera epidemics. The decision
to make it the capital of the
new nation was made for the reason
that most important Canadian
decisions are made: no other choice
seemed possible. Kingston was
too close to the American border,
which then was not unfortified.
Montreal was too "French"; Toronto
too "English". Ottawa had twin
advantages: the Rideau Canal linked
it to Kingston; the river to
Montreal and the St. Lawrence.

Though Ottawa still has a few
surviving relics of its unsightly past,
some of it now is beautiful. The
National Capital Commission's labours
come to slow fruition in public
gardens and landscaped parks.
Lumbermen have given way to civil
servants. The embassies of the
world's nations are here. The tensions
of a tense world are expressed
here in the guarded understatements of
men who know that lives and fortunes
can hang on the words they use.

PARLIAMENT BUILDINGS,
OTTAWA, ONTARIO

Ottawa's climate is Montreal's, only a little more so: its heat-waves in summer are breathless, its winter winds can sear the eyeballs. The city also reflects the broad linguistic divisions of the nation itself: one-third of it is French-speaking. But because its public education is still controlled by Ontario, its French-speaking citizens still must clamour for linguistic equality in their schools.

WELLINGTON STREET, OTTAWA, ONTARIO

Toronto, once the bastion of Britishdom in Canada, has suddenly become her most "ethnic" city, to the vast relief of lovers of good cooking, good music and good theatre. Canada still refrains from turning herself into an ethnic melting pot, her instinct telling her that she can survive only by encouraging human individuality.

KENSINGTON MARKET, TORONTO, ONTARIO

If a Torontonian who had died
fifteen years ago could return to life,
he could not believe this scene
at the Penny Farthing coffee house,
Yorkville. This district, a
block north of Bloor Street,
consists mainly of prettily painted
wooden houses, most of them
turned into smart boutiques and art
galleries. The espresso spots
at night are taken over by beatniks
or simply young people who
like folk-rock and yé-yé.

The great shift in Canadian
morals and mores which began
after the Hitler War is more obvious
in Toronto even than in Montreal.
The traditional puritanism has
cracked wide open – with mixed results.
The New Canadians may turn out
to be the catalytic agents who will
direct this new-found energy
into creative channels. Canada was
luckier than the United States
in the time at which she received the
human flood from the European
continent. The New Canadians who
came here after the Hitler
War, even the working classes, were
educated men and women, the
beneficiaries of the educational
reforms introduced into their native
lands in the twentieth century.

YORKVILLE AVENUE,
TORONTO, ONTARIO

Wish-fulfilment, dream, or prophecy? Here is the Toronto skyline, trick-photographed at night — glittering, cold as ice, asceptic. But Toronto's new City Hall, designed by Viljo Revell, is surely one of the most brilliant and daring in the world, as pure, clean and graceful as mathematics.

LAKEFRONT SKYLINE, TORONTO, ONTARIO

OPPOSITE: CITY HALL, TORONTO, ONTARIO

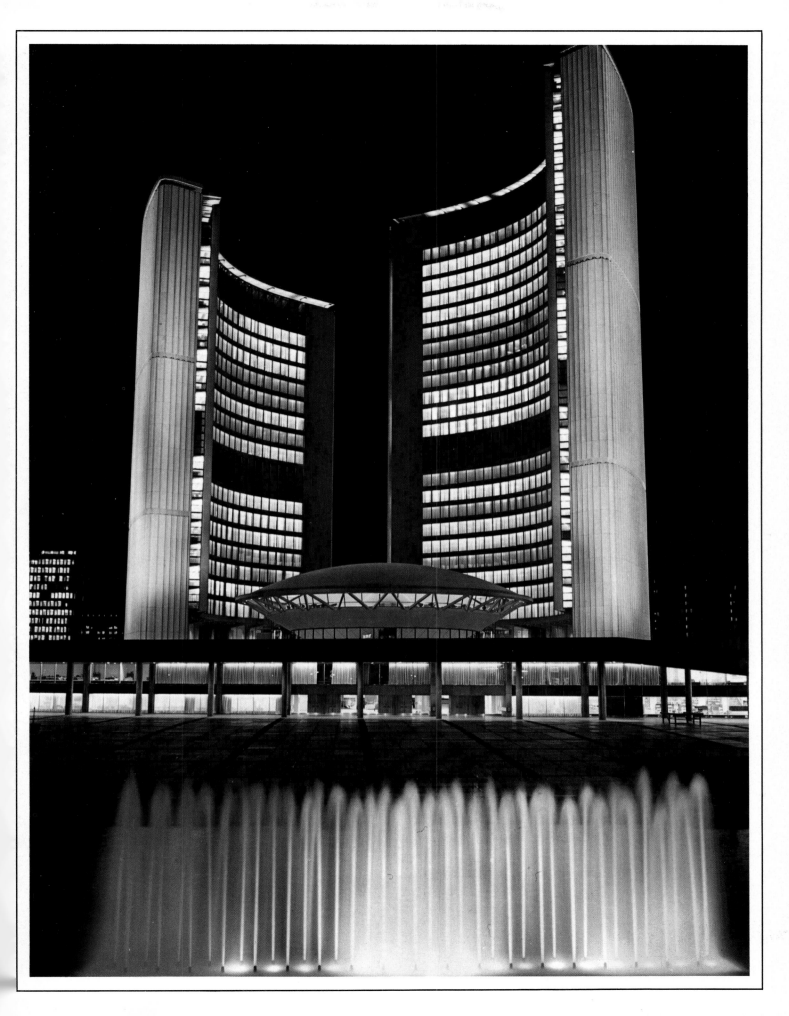

Ontarians are really the most
astonishing people in Canada.
Stratford, for years dependent on
its locomotive factories, its
most famous citizen the hockey player
Howie Morenz, as the result of a
dream in the mind of Tom Patterson,
the genius of Sir Tyrone Guthrie
and the unlocked talents of Canadian
actors from all over the country,
is now the Shakespearean centre of the
continent, with thousands of
people coming from everywhere each
summer season to see the plays
as the Elizabethans saw them. One
leaves the theatre after the
evening performance. The sky is clear,
the people move slowly, the waters
of the Avon reflect the lights:

Look, how the floor of heaven
Is thick inlaid with patines of
bright gold:
There's not the smallest orb which
thou behold'st
But in his motion like an angel
sings...

SHAKESPEAREAN FESTIVAL THEATRE,
STRATFORD, ONTARIO

"And Niagara stuns with thundering sound"...
Goldsmith, who had never seen the Falls, imagined them
in 1770 as one of the horrors awaiting the poor folk expelled from
The Deserted Village *in the time of the British enclosures.*
History, the eternal ironist!

To Canadians from the Maritimes,
Quebec and the Prairies, the
farmland of Ontario seems almost
too good to be true. It is
gentle, rich and rolling, well
watered, soothed by mists
and moisture from the Great Lakes.
In winter it seems asleep,
but rarely are the winters harsh
enough to kill plants. From
thousands of family farms like these
came the young men and women who
fed the province's famous universities.
Conservative as farm-bred people
always are — they know that nature
cannot be rushed and that
forced plants are weak plants — they
have always balanced the restless
drive and change of Toronto,
which may be the provincial capital
but does not yet control the
provincial legislature.

OPPOSITE: KLEINBURG, ONTARIO

The North begins in Ontario at
Georgian Bay, but in summer
it's warm enough for rattlesnakes.
Naked rock formations stand
magnificent against the sky and in
the tremendous autumn storms
the blowing maple leaves stain
the air. It was here that
Tom Thomson and his colleagues of
the Group of Seven first
painted the Canadian northland
as it truly is, and thereby
enabled millions of their countrymen
to see the nature of their land.

GEORGIAN BAY, ONTARIO

The fiftieth parallel of latitude
cuts through the northern part
of Lake Nipigon in the Shield
above Lake Superior — it also
cuts through Penzance, where palm
trees flourish, through the
Somme Department of France, through
Bastôgne, Mainz and Bavaria.
In Europe these are central latitudes;
in Canada, Nipigon is part of
"the North" — spring seasons of
mosquitoes and black flies,
warm summers when the wind is south
but cold when it comes down
from the world's roof, winters colder
than in most parts of Siberia.

Here is the visible legacy of the
Great Glacier, which scraped
bare the earth's bones and gouged out
thousands of basins which now
are lakes. It will always be a
wilderness. Planes, helicopters and
bulldozers open up tiny industrial
settlements in scattered spots, but
the moment the ore-beds are
exhausted, these settlements become
ghost towns. But the North
nevertheless will make Canada
different from any other
modern nation. It is on the edge of
the settled places — the silence
of eternity always within a few hours,
or less, of a technological
civilization.

LAKE NIPIGON, ONTARIO

Vignettes of Ontario:

Patterns of leaves and trees; icicles — frost has come
after thaw; a suburban housing sprawl
produced by those well-known North American twins,
greed and haste; a wind-cracked tree in
farmland; a junk yard; pumpkins that speak for
themselves; interchange of Highways 400
and 401, Toronto — not a ziggurat from the Middle
East, but Scarborough Bluffs, near Toronto.

Across the Prairies

rom Ottawa to the Prairies along the line of the
Canadian Pacific you travel for a night, a day and
most of the night following and nearly all of this
journey is through the empty land of the Shield, the
train wiggling like a mechanical snake around little
lakes, with aspens and spruce blurring past the
windows. Before sunset in summer you reach
Lake Superior and it is like coming upon an ocean.
Port Arthur and Fort William . . . then into the
Shield again and at dawn you are at Kenora and the
Lake-of-the-Woods. Living in a few hours through
that appalling terrain, you may think back and try to
imagine the miracle of the voyageurs who reached

Fort William, birchbark canoes, four tons of trade-goods and 36 portages, in thirty-six to forty days.

Then the rocks thin out. Suddenly you see black earth appearing and then you are in a land-ocean, the black prairie of Manitoba, on the horizon is a grain elevator and the onion dome of a Ukrainian church.

The breaching of the frontier between Ontario and the West is still the greatest achievement in the history of Canada. In this age of masses and abstractions, let it not be forgotten that this was the work of a very few men, that guts and imagination working together are the expression of the Divine in human life.

The Prairies

Not so long ago — perhaps no longer
ago than 15,000 years —
the eastern Canadian prairie lay
under the waters of Lake Agassiz,
which rapidly drained off
into Hudson Bay as the Ice Cap
receded. When the lake still
covered the land, it drained off
through the Great Lakes
and the St. Lawrence. Lake of the
Woods, the Red River and the
prairie lakes — Winnipeg, Winnipegosis,
Manitoba — are its survivals.
So is the black earth of Manitoba,
enriched by thousands of years
of dead and decayed marine life. So,
for that matter, is the
tableflat land itself, crushed by
quadrillions of tons of ice.

A land — sea, flat in Manitoba,
rolling a little in Saskatchewan,
and above it prairie skies
like the one in this picture. Often
when you drive along a prairie
road like this, running straight to
the horizon, you have the illusion
that something is the matter
with your car — that it has become
stationary. When you fly
across it after dark it seems to be
dotted with fireflies —
lights from barns and the windows
of farmhouses, with occasionally
a blaze of light that is a city
or town. This is a land that can best
be described in music, but
the music to describe it has yet
to be written.

THE QUEEN'S HIGHWAY,
SASKATCHEWAN

Wheat for the world, including Russia and China.
From the air, especially in spring, much of the Saskatchewan
prairie resembles a modern art gallery, the rectangular
sectional farms with their curving tree-lines, planted against
erosion, forming the designs, the blue-green of
young wheat contrasting with the dark earth of ploughed land.

HARVEST PATTERNS, SASKATCHEWAN

89

AN ISLAND OF ELEVATORS IN A SEA OF GRAIN

The towns with their grain elevators are like ships
in this land-sea. Also, just as at sea, the weather dominates.
The movement of clouds, their rapid changes of colour,
make the wind visible. When the wheat is ripe, it writhes in
the wind, it boils in the wind, ominously gold under the
darkened sky, Van Gogh's wheatfield near Arles on a colossal scale.

STORM THREATENING OVER THE WHEATLANDS

Who Has Seen The Wind—
the verb is the decisive word in
the title of W. O. Mitchell's
wonderful novel of a boy
growing up on the prairie, discovering
life, love, cruelty, fear
and God in the movement of grain,
in the sound of the wind,
in the prairie birds and animals.
A land which might have produced
Hebraic prophets looking up
to that appalling sky and asking
the Creator, "What is man,
that thou art mindful of him" and
more than once coming to the
conclusion that He is not. Mitchell's
phrase that here life is reduced
to "the common denominator of sky and
Saskatchewan prairie" serves
better than reams of analysis to
explain the feeling of prairie
people that their life is unique,
that the people in the East
and on the Pacific Coast can never
really understand them.
It explains the almost perpetual
political opposition of the
prairie provinces to whatever is the
ruling party in the central
Canadian government.

ABOVE: STORM SKY, THE PRAIRIES;

RIGHT: WHEAT AT HARVEST

Bleak — yes. Yet, so mysterious is beauty, haunting.
The stark word PIONEER is still apt
on this grain elevator on a siding of the trans-
continental railway line which links it to
Montreal and Vancouver. On these plains when
the first settlers came in, the creak of
the wooden wheels in the Red River carts sounded
for miles; then came the lonely wail of the
whistles on the steam locomotives; now, there's the
penetrating blare of the new horns on the Diesels.

ABOVE: HORSES GRAZE THE WESTERN PASTURE

LEFT: TRACKSIDE GRAIN ELEVATORS

Cities of the Plains

Prairie cities — here Edmonton, Winnipeg and Calgary,
and on this day in Calgary there is no sun
and the temperature is fifty below zero, the people
mostly indoors though they have come to work
in their cars. The people — it is in the cities, when
you reach them across the plains, that you begin
to grasp what they have done in such a little time.
Apart from the Red River Settlement,
out of which Fort Garry grew into Winnipeg, all
the development on the Prairies post-dates
Confederation. The inarticulate courage of the pioneers
can scarcely be reached with the imagination.
They came out with their families on the colonist cars —
came out to a land without trees, and therefore
without wood to build shelters. Thousands of them began
their lives in sod huts just as the Russians
did long ago on the steppes. But look at the cities
now! When the oil came in, some of them
possibly got rich too quick. But their universities,
a generation ago lacking in nearly everything,
now teem with students, and some of the best scientists
in the land are in their staffs.

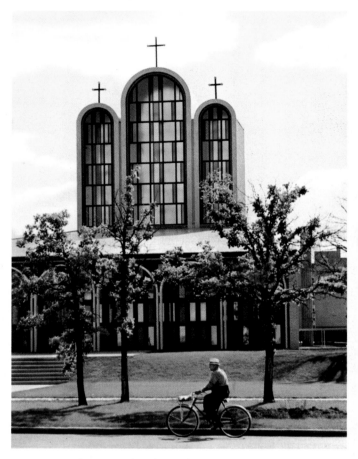

Winnipeg Ukrainian church is rich with stained glass.

Modern sculpture accents new City Hall at Edmonton.

In Edmonton's east end, at an intersection of Jasper.

Eighty-two degrees of frost puts a rime on Calgary. A century ago, here at the Bow River there was only a police post.

A comic, irreverent note: contour contrasts on Winnipeg's Main Street.

A new parking garage for Edmonton's affluent society.

An inlet at Outlook, Saskatchewan, for the Qu'Appelle barrage.

Window wall in Regina, Sask.: the Power Corporation Building.

When you travel across the far western prairie the dramatic moment
comes, not when you see the skyline of the Rockies, but
when you reach the visible tilt where the prairie begins to rise.
This moment does not come until you have passed the
110th parallel of longitude — farther south, in Colorado, the
moment arrives some eight parallels of longitude farther east,
the Canadian prairie being wider than the American because the
Rockies swerve easterly south of the border. At Calgary
the foothills begin, rolling like the smaller waves that herald
the moment of the titanic seas of a hurricane.
Beyond them the earth-waves are grey, minaretted, the earth
in tempest all the way to the Pacific.

WILD FLOWERS IN THE ALBERTAN FOOTHILLS

British Columbia

The natural division between the Prairies and the cordilleran West is the most dramatic of them all. The Great Divide in the so-called Canadian Rockies marks the line of demarcation between Alberta and British Columbia. This is the range of mountains which separates the waters flowing easterly to reach the Atlantic through Hudson Bay, and westerly to reach the Pacific. In the case of the Peace and Athabasca rivers, the waters drain through the Mackenzie Basin to the Artic. The Columbia Icefield, straddling the Divide, is the source of major rivers which reach all three oceans.

The piercing of the vast ranges of the British Columbia mountains by the railways was Canada's greatest single response to the physical challenge of her environment. The success of Confederation depended upon it. In our time, the bulldozer has

enabled the magnificently scenic Trans-Canada
Highway to make it possible for automobiles to pass
through the ranges on comfortable grades all the
way to the coast.

    Among the wisest acts ever performed by federal
parliament were the ones which created the national
parks—Waterton Lakes (which is part of the
International Peace Park straddling the U.S. border),
Banff, Yoho, Jasper, Kootenay and others. Though
Banff and Jasper are technically in Alberta, they
belong to the cordilleran region of the Canadian West.
Here, if nowhere else on this progressive continent,
the balance of nature still holds. Elk, moose,
deer, antelope, bears black and grizzly, marmots,
and other rodents, even wolves, live without
fear of the hunter and anyone can see them
who visits the parks.

British Columbia

THE CANADIAN CORDILLERAS: THE DIVIDE BETWEEN ALBERTA AND BRITISH COLUMBIA

When the English poet Rupert Brooke visited the Rockies just
before the 1914-18 War, he made a poet's remark that still
can be used to put them into perspective: "I missed the voices
of the dead." Some Canadians at the time were offended,
including Prime Minister Borden, who said so in print.
He should have known better. Over a period of thousands of years,
Europeans learned to live in the Alps, to live with them:
to create a special architecture, to clear mountain meadows for
the pasture of sheep and goats; even to fight wars in them.
Our Rockies are still prehistoric.

British Columbia's rivers are the most spectacular
on the continent. The incredible Fraser, charging down
the Rocky Mountain Trench, bending around
the Cariboo, confined in its canyon all the way down
to Hope, passing tranquilly through the nation's
most beautiful farmed valley into its delta, issuing in
the Georgia Strait, is as long as the Rhine and is
the greatest salmon breeder in the world. Here we see
the Thompson, named after the geographer of
the North West Company. At Lytton it smashes into the Fraser
like a liquid battering ram, blue water sharp
against the Fraser's brown, then is swallowed and disappears.

THOMPSON RIVER, BRITISH COLUMBIA

The Kootenay, four hundred miles long,
rises in the B.C. Rockies, flows south into Montana and
Idaho, then bends north and returns to Canada
to enter Kootenay Lake, a lake seventy-five miles long,
so magnificent that the only word fit to describe
it is its own name. Leaving the lake, it discharges into
the Columbia, which flows south across the American border.
The character of these mountain rivers is schizophrenic:
where the drop is rapid and they are confined, they are raging
torrents of incalculable power; wherever the flow slackens, they
are tranquil vistas of water reflecting the sky.

KOOTENAY RIVER, BRITISH COLUMBIA

ABOVE: TOTEM POLES AT PRINCE RUPERT, BRITISH COLUMBIA

OPPOSITE: FIRS IN GARIBALDI PARK, BRITISH COLUMBIA

Civilization in its early stages resulted from inertia: the invention of agriculture stopped nomadic habits and pinned the people long enough in one place to enable them to foster crafts and arts. On the British Columbia coast the abundance of salmon played this role. It held the people to the river mouths. When Alexander Mackenzie encountered the Indians of the coast he marvelled at their art, but even more did he marvel at their skill with canoes. He said they were superior to his own voyageurs, the ultimate accolade.

The Douglas firs of British Columbia, some of them, are more than a thousand years old. In the Redpath Museum of McGill University is a cross section of one of them, its inner rings indicating its age. When it first began to grow, Alfred the Great was King of England.

Among some primitive cultures (not confined
to the New World by any means) the individual
human being was supposed to have a mystical,
or even a real, relationship to some animal,
plant, bird or inanimate object. Whatever this
was became his totem. The man might be
a descendant of his totem, or the two might be
descended from a common ancestor. The man
might be prohibited from killing or eating the
animal, bird or plant that is his totem.
A group or a tribe, or parts of different tribes,
might have the same totem and be prohibited
from marriage within the totem kin. Nowhere have
such magnificent specimens of totem art
survived as in the coast of British Columbia.
The genius of the painter Emily Carr
has distilled the essence and beauty of them,
together with their mysterious meaning.

ABOVE: THUNDERBIRD PARK,
VICTORIA, BRITISH COLUMBIA

LEFT: A FALLEN TOTEM AT KISPIOX,
BRITISH COLUMBIA

Vancouver, the western terminus of
the railway lines that made
Canada a nation, on the sheltered
waters of the Georgia Strait,
its site discovered in the
eighteenth century by the British
naval explorer Captain George
Vancouver, has the most enviable
future of any city in Canada.
It has grown with astonishing
speed from a small lumber
town into Canada's third-largest
city. The measure of its
growth, in terms of time, can be seen
in the University of British
Columbia situated on a peninsula
jutting out into the Strait.
As late as 1917, this was still
a branch of McGill's Extension
Department; now it is the second-
largest university in
the land, and still growing.

The buildings in this picture
are brand-new. Here is the
esthetically justifiable use of
the high-rise, at least for
the tenants with a seaward view.
When one comes to Vancouver
and looks around, one feels like
saying a prayer to its citizens:
"You can make this city a
western Athens if you wish it to
become immortal, and not a bonanza
for real estate speculation.
Please, please do it!"

HIGH-RISE APARTMENTS,
VANCOUVER,
BRITISH COLUMBIA

Here the engineers and planners have not failed. The Lions Gate Bridge perfectly combines utility with art, which always conspires with nature. At night, in fog, or in sun, this bridge never lets its setting down. It never seeks to impose itself upon its surroundings. It becomes part of them, and by so doing, helps to define them.

LIONS GATE BRIDGE, VANCOUVER, BRITISH COLUMBIA

Stanley Park has an aquarium, a small zoo with native animals and reptiles, gardens, flowering shrubs and giant trees. Salt water laps its shores; in fog it is mysterious; in fine weather the sun filters through the branches as in this picture. But its mood is natural, and what men have done to improve it does not obtrude on its wonderful natural setting. It is a pleasant thought that the seaward tip of Canada's Atlantic port, Halifax, is also a natural park, though there the trees are nearly all spruce and pines, and in winter it is cold. It never seems cold in Stanley Park. The air is soft as it is in Cornwall and the climate much the same.

OPPOSITE: STANLEY PARK,
VANCOUVER, BRITISH COLUMBIA

Early morning fog swirls across Vancouver Harbour.

Winter in Vancouver's 900-acre Stanley Park.

On the waterfront, Vancouver.

North Vancouver photographed from an aircraft at
nine thousand feet: the Coast Mountains dusted with snow;
Lynn and Seymour Canyons striking up through
the ranges on the right; left-centre, the line of the chair
lift going up the side of Grouse Mountain;
in the docks, ships bound for any port on the Pacific.

The sheltered waters of Georgia Strait, with Vancouver Island acting as a gigantic breakwater against the ocean surges, is almost perfect for yachting and small-boat cruising. In the outer harbour small boys can learn to sail in dinghies. Larger craft have the prospect of the whole British Columbia coast.

YACHT CLUB, WEST VANCOUVER, BRITISH COLUMBIA
OPPOSITE: IN VANCOUVER HARBOUR, BRITISH COLUMBIA

The spectacular indentations of the coastline about Vancouver spare the citizens from the curious melancholy that affects people (whether they know it or not) who live facing an uninterrupted horizon on a western ocean—the sight of the setting sun being swallowed in the sea as though it had perished out of the world. Here the setting sun haloes promotories and islands.

Vancouver Island—285 miles long, in places 3,000 feet high, coastline indented by deep inlets; moist Pacific winds; unspoiled streams plentiful in salmon and steelhead; small lakes in the interior; orchards, farms, lumber mills and beaches.

ABOVE: ENGLISH BAY, VANCOUVER, BRITISH COLUMBIA
RIGHT: ON LONG BEACH, VANCOUVER ISLAND, BRITISH COLUMBIA

Victoria, capital of British
Columbia, was founded in
1843 as a Hudson's Bay Company's
trading post known as
Fort Camosun, later renamed
Victoria in honour of
the Queen. Its suburb, Esquimalt,
is the eastern base of the
Canadian Navy. It became the capital
of the province in 1866,
one year before Canadian
Confederation and five years before
British Columbia joined Canada
as the sixth province (one year after
Manitoba). When we remember
that, in 1870, Victoria was divided
from "Canada" by more than
two thousand miles of Shield country,
prairies almost empty of
humanity, by hundreds of miles of
mountains, the boldness of
this decision takes the breath away.
As a Canadian newspaper
recently pointed out, if computers had
existed a century ago such a decision
would never have been made.
All the evidence that men could
have fed into it would have
said "no" to it . . .

OPPOSITE:

PARLIAMENT BUILDINGS,

VICTORIA, BRITISH COLUMBIA

RIGHT:

THE WESTERN OCEAN,

FROM VANCOUVER ISLAND,

BRITISH COLUMBIA

The journey ends

The cameras have come to the end of a journey
which began in Newfoundland and ended in
Vancouver Island. They have tried to follow
the long thread of settlement from coast to
coast. They have omitted most of Canada; how
could they possibly have included more than
a minuscule suggestion of the enormous land?

We live in a world so cursed by the
inspirational messages of professional phrase-
makers, commercial and political, that we
have bred a young generation whose ears are
sealed even to the truth if the truth is
optimistic. We live in a world so stupefied
and confused by scientific surveys, opinion
polls, computerized predictions that most of us
for the sake of our sanity make our separate
peace-pacts with these insensate abstractions.
In Canada we are still asking ourselves the
question, "Who are we?" It would be better to
look at what we are and what the nation has
done in so short a time.

In the Funeral Oration delivered by
Pericles to the Athenians more than four
hundred years before Christ, he made the
classic understatement: "Our city is superior
to the report of her."

Canada would not look like much if she were
merely superior to the report of her given
by a lot of her citizens. The fact is that her
record is almost incredible. Now after a
long winter of subterranean growth, her artists
and writers, musicians and dancers are
beginning to express her meaning not only to
their own people but to the outside world.
She is joining articulate civilization and is
earning her right to do so.

The photography in this book was done by:

«Roloff Beny»

«Robert Brooks»

«Ted Czolowski»

«Rene Delbuguet»

«Horst Ehricht»

«George Hunter»

«Albert Krafczyk»

«Jack Long»

«Malak»

«Bill McKay»

«Farley Mowat»

«Don Newlands»

«Eberhard Otto»

«Gordon Reeve»

«Peter Varley»

«John De Visser»

«Doug. Wilkinson»

Picture Credits

Order of appearance in the text of pictures listed here is left to right, top to bottom. After the first recording, principal sources are credited under these abbreviations:

RB	Roloff Beny
BB	Bob Brooks
JDV	John de Visser
HE	Horst Ehricht
GH	George Hunter
JL	Jack Long
M	Malak
M, MS	Malak, from Miller Services
DN	Don Newlands
EEO, MS	Eberhard E. Otto (from Miller Services)

Page	Credit
COVER	Albert Krafczyk
2-3	John de Visser
7	Gerald Campbell
13	Doug Wilkinson; Farley Mowat
14	George Hunter
16-17	Walter Bonatti
18-19	Doug Wilkinson
22	Roloff Beny
23	RB
24-25	Malak (from Miller Services)
26	JDV
27	JDV
28	Peter Varley
29	Horst Ehricht
30	HE
31	PV
32-33	RB
34	RB
35	RB
36	M, MS
37	Bob Brooks
38	HE
39	HE
40-41	M, MS
42	BB; BB; BB; BB
43	BB
46-47	Eberhard E. Otto (from Miller Services)
48-49	HE
50	JDV
51	JDV
52-53	Rene Delbuguet
54-55	JDV
56	JDV; JDV; JDV; JDV
57	JDV; JDV; JDV; JDV
58	JDV
59	JDV
60-61	GH
62	RB
63	M, MS; M; MS;
66-67	EEO, MS
68	RB
69	PV
70-71	HE
72	JDV
73	Bill McKay (from Miller Services)
74-75	GH
76-77	EEO, MS
78	GH; M
79	Gordon Reeve
80-81	Ont. Dept. of Tourism and Information
82	PV; PV; JDV; JDV; JDV
83	JDV; Ont. Dept. of Highways; JDV; JDV; RB; JDV
86-87	JDV
88-89	M
90	M
91	HE
92	HE
93	M
94	RB
95	RB
96	HE; HE; HE
97	RB
98	HE; HE; RB
99	HE
100-101	PV
102	RB
103	RB
106-107	PV; PV
108	Jack Long
109	RB
110	PV
111	HE
112-113	Don Newlands
114	DN
115	JL
116	JL
117	JL; JL; JL
118-119	VREB-Czolowski
120	JL
121	JL
122	JL
123	DN
124	GH
125	DN
126	DN

The type-face chosen for this book is Deepdene, set in Canada by Mono Lino Typesetting Co. Ltd.
The book was printed and bound in Italy by Arnoldo Mondadori, Officine Grafiche.